MW01230964

With love

Olinda Daniels

Alinda C Daniels

# RHYMES
## FROM
## THE HEART

# RHYMES FROM THE HEART

iUniverse books may be ordered through booksellers or by contacting:

iUniverse
1663 Liberty Drive
Bloomington, IN 47403
www.iuniverse.com
1-800-Authors (1-800-288-4677)

ISBN: 978-1-5320-7466-0 (sc)
ISBN: 978-1-5320-7468-4 (hc)
ISBN: 978-1-5320-7467-7 (e)

Print information available on the last page.

iUniverse rev. date: 05/10/2019

# Contents

# The Day Before Dawn

It's the Day before Dawn in a room dim and bleak
A frail, gentle man lay so humble and meek.
His once mighty frame now slowly inches away
And his coal, black hair now has a touch of grey.

His heart of gold still beats hard and strong
But despair in his eyes depict something's wrong.
His strong, loving hands once worked with great pride
Now these weak, tender hands lay gently by his side.

His voice is silent, no words ever spoken
His movements are few, his stride has been broken.
He's just as helpless as a small, weary child
Depending on his "*FATHER*" to carry him a while.

It's a quite afternoon and a warm, July day
Silence is broken in a most unusual way.
His eyes fill with tears that flow down his cheeks
His bottom lip trembles, still unable to speak.

His once lifeless arms stretch out in mid air
Responding as if someone special was there.
His unspoken words are clearly seen --
This is real to him, it isn't a dream.

There's a change taking place within these walls
He's getting ready to answer the call.
It's a quiet afternoon - the Day Before Dawn
When God's Holy Angels come to take Daddy home.

*aDc*
*08/13/82*

# The Bus Stop

School Days, School Days . . . it's that time of year
Up bright and early, the hour is almost here.
Wiping the sleep from my eyes, I soon can see
God granted my wish -- some sunshine for me!

Greeted by my pal, you know . . . Captain Crunch
We sit down for breakfast, I like him a bunch!
Hurry to the dresser to comb and brush my hair;
Got to be ready 'cause the bus will soon be here.

Mama's in the kitchen, Daddy's gone to work
Little brother is mama's shadow tugging on her skirt.
Not quite ready to spread his wings and fly
I whisper "I love you" and hug and kiss goodbye.

Out the door, down the road, I'm off to meet the bus
Kicking at the pebbles, stirring up some dust.
Waiting and looking as far as I can see
Look! Here comes the bus - it's coming just for me.

ACD
07/01/96

# Stranger Within

Come hither my child, come go with me
Come hold my hand, come sit on my knee.
I'll tell you some stories, I'll give you some treats
We'll sing some songs, we'll play hide and seek.

We'll listen for the birds and watch for the bees
We'll have lots of fun, just wait and see!
Just think of the good times we can share
Come go with me – I'll show you I care.

Let me take you to a place where dreams come true
There's something very special just waiting for you.
Just give me your hand, he said with a smile
As he whisked her away – this trusting little child.

All too often this story's been told
It's never ending and never grows old.
The innocence of childhood has now been stolen
This trusting little heart has cruelly been broken.

aDc
07/01/96

# I Am Me!

*I am Me – One of Many, but only one you'll see.*
*So, don't expect of me someone I cannot be.*
*I might be a giddy child of four or a toddler of two;*
*But until you take close notice, I'll be who you see to you.*

*Perhaps a quiet little boy of six feeling weak and thin*
*Looking for my sister – my flesh and blood - my twin.*
*Or I might be a private eye on a hot, mysterious trail*
*Or a tiny little baby so fragile and so frail.*

*I might even be a dancer twirling in mid air*
*Or a lady of the night with that sophisticated flair.*
*Could be Susie Tomboy kicking snakes and snails*
*Or a lonely twelve-year-old letting out a whail.*

*Perhaps an old grouch choosing to be alone*
*Or the one who got away and now is gone.*
*How 'bout "Miss Prim and Proper," elegant and neat*
*Or "Mr. Know It All" sometimes known as Pete!*

*I know who I am, both inside and out*
*And I know we love "us all", there's no doubt.*
*So, judge me not when I am near, and yet far away*
*Just accept me today...tomorrow...and love me always!*

*aDc*
*05/21/00*

# The Library

*Tiny little Book of Secrets resting on the shelf*
*Filling up some empty space where only dust was left.*
*Secrets of the morning, secrets of yesterday*
*Secrets that linger on and on and never go away.*

*Tiny little Book of Tears resting just next door*
*With washed out pages tucked inside keeping all the scores.*
*Tear stained letters streaking down each page*
*Some filled with emotions, some consumed with rage.*

*Tiny little Book of Memories located two books down*
*Holding thoughts of childhood yet scattered all around.*
*Dreams of yesterdays that started as tomorrows*
*Escaping to another place from which in time we borrow.*

*Tiny Little Puzzle Book next in line to see*
*Filled with gaping timelines and senseless mysteries.*
*Questions still unanswered - just some empty space*
*A quest to anyone to put the pieces in their place.*

*Next, a Little Diary takes up a tiny block*
*Just some private thoughts secured within a little lock.*
*Perhaps a blushing thought or two about the boy next door*
*Perhaps a mention of the first kiss that swept one off the floor.*

*So here's My Little Library that I hold within my heart*
*It's meaningless to anyone else but, to me, a vital part.*
*It's a gateway to the past, and a portal to what lies ahead*
*It's the key to understanding the thoughts within my head.*

*And when I take a journey to heal my wounded soul*
*I like me for who I am and seek a rewarding goal.*
*Those puzzles get easier every day, as simple as 1, 2, 3*
*And then I finally realize who this is that I call "ME."*

aDc
05/30/98

# All I Want For Christmas . . .

Dear Mr. Santa:

Here's my list of dreams and special wishes, too
All written down and sealed with love especially for you
You see, a dolly I want not, nor a wagon or a train
I neither want a bicycle, nor a locket on a chain.

My biggest wish would be for Christmases past
With fondest memories that would forever last.
I would wish that my daddy be your helper again
And momma right beside him, cozy in the den.

I would want to hear the laughter of everyone at play
And wait for the snow to fall making it a perfect day.
A little bit of heaven, a whole lot of peace on earth
A joyous celebration of Jesus' truly amazing birth.

But now my wish list consist of impossible things
Yesteryears of memories when we would dance and sing.
Then as fate would take its place, my world began to die
And Santa, they can't re-appear no matter how hard you try.

'Tis the season for laughter, for songs and for praise
And wonderful loved-ones to celebrate the holidays!
So, All I Want for Christmas is a peaceful heart within
Overflowing with joy and excitement...
                    Please bring that back again!

A Daniels
12/13/99
05:00 am

11

# Crafty Lady

Sitting in my parlor in my easy chair
Bedroom slippers on my feet, curlers in my hair,
Thinking of something to occupy my time
Maybe something easy in which I''ll do just fine.

Tried the art of knitting, it threw me for a whirl
Couldn't keep the stitches right between a knit and a purl.
Finally made a scarf that fit me to a tee
Kept me good and warm, all the way down to my knee!

So then to macrame, I thought I would try
Got so twisted in the turns, thought I'd surely die.
Finally made a hanger in which my plants could rest.
This is not my cup of tea, I really must confess.

So on to crochet, although I did debate
But one less needle to use and this sounded great!
I'll finish this project this time, I bet;
Got an afghan in my closet, it "ain't" finished yet.

On to something different, how about some art I'll do
Didn't know there were so many shades of blue.
My first painting was supposed to be a vase
But, as luck would have it, it had no base.

Guess I'll stick to what I do best
Be a mom and housewife and leave the rest.
I've tried them all – I'm not "afraidy"
Just don't call me a crafty lady!

aDc
03/02/2019

13

# Little One . . .

*What's a life without memories and dreams to share?*
*What's a childhood without that gentle, loving care?*
*Just a deep, dark void - Not making any sense*
*Filled with make-believe dreams of fake pretense.*

*Oh for a moment of truth unveiled*
*Oh my soul! Where all that is . . . has failed.*
*The innocence of the young now lays by the way*
*Seeking gentleness in the light of a new day.*

*A little one, alone, knowing not of a heart betrayed*
*Only the feeling of loneliness and being afraid.*
*Knowing not the stars are bright, the sun so warm;*
*The promise of tomorrow - without a cloud or storm!*

*Oh little one - so young, so tender, so sweet*
*Dry the tears from your eyes, the drops from your cheeks.*
*Hold on to your dreams - there's so much more*
*A world of wonder waiting behind that locked door!*

*Hold on to tomorrow, for there is joy yet to feel!*
*It's wonderful, it's exciting, and, yes, it is real.*
*The racing of your heart, the tingling deep inside;*
*Don't run from these feelings - there's no need to hide.*

*They're just emotions finding their way to the top;*
*They've been hidden so long, don't ask them to stop!*
*All these feelings make up All that you are;*
*Now it's time to heal the wounds and mend the scars.*

*It's true . . . "It's always darkest just before dawn"*
*The road may be rough, so be patient and strong*
*Just hold on tight, catch hold of the beam*
*It's time to make real those "make-believe" dreams!*

*Good Luck, Little One!*

*aDc ("Lindy") 10/25/95*

# In Loving Memory

Your gentle face and patient smile
With sadness we recall.
You had a kindly word for each
And died beloved by all.

The voice is mute and stilled the heart
That loved us well and true.
Ah, bitter was the trial to part
From one so good as you.

You are not forgotten loved one
Nor will you ever be.
As long as life and memory last
We will remember thee.

We miss you now, our hearts are sore
As time go by we miss you more.
Your loving smile and gentle face
No one can ever fill your vacant place.

aDc
07/23/83

# If Walls Could Talk

*If only we could speak our mind*
*What tales of tales*
*we'd leave behind!*

*We'd tell of all the scandalous lies*
*And cover-up of our*
*children's cries.*
*The thought of gaining*
*a cherished trust*
*Is mere a chance and not a must.*

*We'd tell of all the shh's and hush*
*And "Let's be quite . . .*
*Don't make a fuss."*
*The confidence both*
*gained and lost*
*Can somehow be used for*
*just the right cost.*

*We'd tell of those whose*
*path we've trod*
*Who sometimes feel they're*
*"Way above GOD."*
*Of those who think that*
*"Up's" the way*
*And doesn't care who has to pay.*

*We'd tell of Leaders*
*who often mislead*
*Because of much desired*
*wealth and greed.*
*It matters not which truth to hold*
*But who can fill their*
*pockets of gold.*

*We'd tell of broken*
*hearts and pain*
*And how the silence*
*does still remain.*
*The price that was paid*
*for a job well done*
*The mark of victory or*
*the hand of shun.*

*We've protected those*
*who seek our room*
*To escape the harshness*
*of a day of gloom.*
*We've wrapped ourselves*
*around many needs*
*And listened to earnest*
*and heartfelt pleas.*

*We're mighty Walls of*
*well kept secrets*
*And unlimited woes and regrets.*
*We've shared the ups*
*and downs of all*
*And watched some rise*
*and watched some fall.*

*No one can know the*
*weight We bear*
*Or hear our cries of hope and care.*
*We're just some walls*
*of dust and chalk*
*But 'Oh what we could*
*tell if only . . .*
**We Could Talk!**

*aDc 04/02/90*
*(rev 04/10/95)*

# Unconditionally

As I strolled along the sidewalks
On a brisk December day
A tiny little toy shop
Seemed to echo sounds my way.

What is this sound I ask
On which my ear had fallen?
Could it be the whispering wind
This stranger it was calling?

As I slowly walked toward the shop
I noticed all the toys.
So many wonderful creations
For all the girls and boys!

But way back in the corner
Was a tattered, broken doll
Hidden from the outside world
Never to evolve.

Her big, brown eyes so sad
They gazed into my heart.
She caught my full attention
Right from the very start

I ask the toy maker
"How much does she cost?"
He said, "I cannot sell her
Her worth is all but lost.

She's very old, my dear,
No life in her I see..
Passed around from home to home,
So, I just let her be.

Her Clothes are torn and ragged
And the glow has left her face,
So the quiet, little corner
Seems to be her proper place.

"But she's something quite unusual,"
He said with a candid grin.
"She's been a good companion
And a true and loving friend.

She's been a great part of my life
A great loss it would be for me
For no one could love her
As I have, UNCONDITIONALLY!"

aDc
03/02/2019

# A Tribute To . . .

MOM

*GOD gave me a special person to love forever and ever*
*Someone who could return that love beyond any measure.*
*She's my best of friends, loyal through and through*
*She always listens and weeps with me when I'm blue.*

*She's my leaning post when I'm faced with life's trials*
*She lifts me up with her gentle hands and a smile.*
*She's the foundation of what I am today*
*She gave me my identity and no can take that away.*

*She's my ray of sunshine when days are dark and bleak*
*She chases clouds away and puts a blush in my cheeks.*
*She's a tower of inspiration to face each coming day*
*She will never leave me . . . even when she's away.*

*We've had some good times and we've had some bad*
*We've shared much laughter; and, too, been sad.*
*But through it all, we've survived just fine;*
*Thanks, Mom, for being there and sharing your time.*

**Happy Mother's Day 5/08/94**
*Alinda*

# Only In A . . .

**O**nly in a lifetime can we find true friends
nly in a dream can we enter the world of pretend
nly in a moment of fleeing minutes and hours
nly God can show us what is to be ours.

**N**ow is the second to hold on to, to live, and to play
ow is the minute to be thankful for each and every day
ow is the hour to count your blessings bestowed to you
ow is the perfect time to give God His dues.

**L**isten to your heart and hear what it has to say
isten to your inner soul that ultimately leads the way
isten to your mind as thoughts of life rush by
isten to God speaking "With me, you will never die"

**Y**ou can live with riches untold or you can pass them by
ou can live forever or you can fade away and die
ou can have a grand reunion or never see "them" again
ou can't have it both ways . . . either life in Christ or sin!

Written by
A.Daniels
06/28/2006

# Decisions

Decisions are made each and every day
Some are easy, some kept at bay.
But making the right one is so hard to do
Answers not only affect others, but also you.
You cannot dismiss a decision, it won't go away
It'll be there no matter what comes your way.
It's tough I know, I've been there too
I've walked a mile in another's shoes'
The best way to decide is to ask God's help
He's always there…He'll guide your step.
He will never leave or ignore you that's true
You just have to give to Him what is due.
Just listen to Him as He softly speaks
Within your heart as it faintly beats.
An answer is waiting if you just listen to it
Don't you ever give up or decide to quit.

aDc
04/18/2019

# The Reunion

*The "Family" reunion was our annual tradition*
*Everyone was expected there under no condition*
*And the times were great and food divine*
*It seemed that everyone had a great time.*

*But, have you ever stopped and wondered how it all began?*
*Who begat who? And, oh yes, who's that man?*
*Just another face to try and remember . . .*
*Is that friend or foe, or another family member?*

*Our reunions began with George Grant and Maude Lee.*
*A gentle papa and a mamma stubborn as she could be.*
*But sweet they were as they grew old together*
*And many grandchildren around them would gather.*

*Then down through time, our family began to fade*
*When someone special was taken away.*
*But as time would have it, a new generation took hold.*
*A strong generation so crazy and bold!*

*Now it's the "Cousins' Reunion" still doing the same*
*Trying to remember the new babies' names.*
*And greeting the cousins not seen in a while*
*With a handshake, a hug, and a big smile.*

*We eat our portion of food provided*
*Never feeling restrained or slighted.*
*We share our stories of fun and laughter*
*And finally retreat home happily-ever-after.*

*aDc*
*03/03/2019*

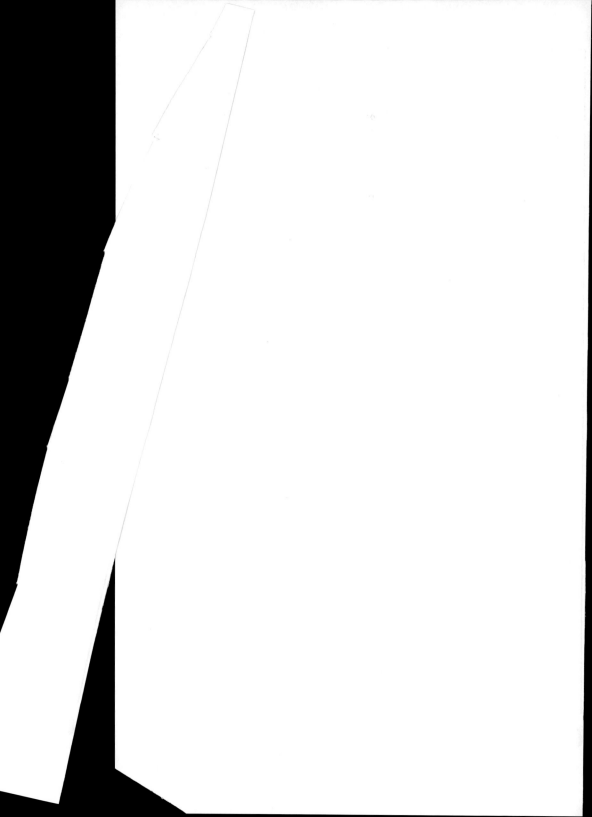

# You're A God Send!

*Little did I know that I would need someone to tell it all to*
*And little did I know that God would lead me to You.*
*You're that special someone that God put in my plans*
*He knew that someday I would be placed in your hands.*
*To Him, nothing was hidden - my life was an open book*
*But to me, it was such a secret and I had forgotten to look!*
*God knew the perfect person to help me begin to heal*
*And He knew the perfect time to break the seal.*

*The journey into my past began some time ago*
*Sometimes it seems so short, and, yet, it seems so slow.*
*The memories are coming, painful as they may be*
*But I have learned more about the little ones that I call, "ME".*
*You've been quite annoying and pushy at times*
*But I must admit - you have been remarkably patient and kind.*
*You've really got a "knack" and two good listening ears*
*And always ready with those kleenex for me to dry my tears.*

*Well, I'm glad I had the chance to meet you and You meet me*
*You see, thanks to you, we know who we are and who we be!*
*This is like a Christmas gift – we've never been able to share*
*It's truly a blessing to know that there are those who really care.*
*So, to you and yours, we wish you glad tidings and good health*
*May friends and family be your strength and your wealth!*
*Hope you have a wonderful holiday and a fantastic good year*
*And Thanks ever so much for just Being Here!*

***Merry Christmas!***
***DR. J***

# The Gift of Life

Ok Mom, you work with all your strife
To bring this baby into life.
At last a little boy appears
All to show his little rear!

Yes, it's a little angel I can hold in my arms,
To cuddle and love, to keep from all harm.
The journey for you just begins
As I proudly present you to my friends.

Here's Little Joe I say to the world
Yes, he's a he and not a girl.
With cheeks so red and eyes so blue
Yep, just like his dad – that is true!

Note no hair upon his head
Only a mist of fuzz instead.
Little fingers, tiny toes
Cute as a button with that pug nose.

He keeps me busy long hours of night
Fighting sleep with all his might.
Yes, I'm still under a lot of strife
To make sure I can raise this "Gift of Life."

aDc
04/18/2019

# Dear Ho Ho.

Just a note to let you know it's true
I know exactly who you are and exactly what you do!
I'm all grown up it seems – there's no turning about;
But let it be known – I still believe in you – no doubt!

I know your habits and I know what you like best
So, don't try to trick me – this isn't a test.
You're at your best when you work with all your might
You work long, hard hours – sometimes late into the night.

You delight in fulfilling wishes of all the girls and boys
You relish with satisfaction when you see their tears of joy.
But sometimes those wishes are just impossible to meet
So, you leave something special and then you retreat.

You're a wonder of wonders – a joy to know
A man of the holidays, well suited for snow.
So, after the season, take a much needed rest
And know within your heart that You've done your very best!

Merry Christmas &
I Love You Ho Ho!

aDc
12/13/99
04:20 am

# Hide 'N Seek

Just as a kid would play, I now hide away
To be alone and escape the hustle of the day.
I got my favorite place and reminisce
Of favorite times and joys amiss.
The solitude amongst the trees is so tranquil
I've found my place of which I am thankful.
The enchanting glow of evening's light
Reminds me of the perfect night.
To rest my thoughts within my head
As I curl up in my cozy bed.
I now and then might take a peek
And go back and play "Hide 'N Seek".

aDc
04/18/2019

# Today I Marry My Friend

*As I stand before you on this wonderful day*
*I have so much to tell you - so much to say.*
*Fondest memories we have shared in the past*
*Wonderful beginnings that will last and last.*

*The little things you say and do*
*Are the reasons I fell in love with you!*
*From the sentimental moments we shared on a date*
*To that special sunset we watched on the lake.*

*The first time you held my hand in yours*
*It gave me strength and courage to open new doors.*
*I cherish our quiet moments at the Y-Beach*
*And feel secure knowing you were there at arm's reach.*

*The dinners, the flowers - even the nutter butters*
*Just more precious memories to add to the others*
*The hugs, the kisses, the dreams we share*
*You make everything special just because you care.*

*Your support... your love... your unselfish time*
*All these and more make me glad you're mine.*
*You're my reason for waking each bright new day*
*You've touched my heart in such a special way.*

*And, now, as we join our lives together*
*May GOD grant us wisdom and strength forever.*
*May HE bless us with little ones to extend our love*
*And may HE always watch over us from up above.*

*As time goes by and we're both old and gray*
*I shall always remember my friend of yesterday.*
*And just as a rose needs the early morning dew*
*I would be nothing without this love from you.*

*I love you so much -- I can't possibly express*
*The joy I feel, the overwhelming happiness!*
*YOU <u>are</u> my STRENGTH, my LOVE, my LIFE*
*And I am so HONORED to become your wife.*

# Letter To God

I wish I had a penny
For every Word of prayer
To remind me constantly
That You are always there.

The road get rough along the way
And I stumble and I fall
But somehow, some way I land on foot
Standing upright and very tall.

You are my God, my soul to seek
You help me along the way
You build me up to heights unknown
You help me face another day.

Thank you for your love and mercy
The constant companion you've become
Never more to leave me here
But gently and safely guide me home.

Love,
Alinda

aDc
04/18/2019

# 'Twas The Month . . .

*'Twas the month before your birthday*
*And all through the House*
*All the children were sleeping --*
*Yes, even my Spouse!*
*The excitement of your Birthday,*
*A promise still to keep . . .*
*Left me wide-eyed and restless*
*And unable to sleep.*

*Sitting in my parlor*
*In my favorite easy chair,*
*My mind began to wander,*
*Fingers nestled through my hair.*
*The thoughts were oh so many -*
*Not seeming to end --*
*What on earth would I . . . could I*
*Get for you - MY FRIEND?*

*Something soft and delicate?*
*Something nice to smell?*
*Something to add to your collection?*
*Oh Well, Well, Well!*
*Would it be some Cross Stitch*
*To hang upon your wall?*
*Should it be big and bold*
*Or something dainty and small?*

*Still pondering over the perfect gift,*
*My thoughts went ever so deep --*
*How about a book of "Memories"*
*That will be yours - Forever To Keep.*
*So to You My Friend, My Sister --*
*The One in Whom I Confide,*
*I hope you'll enjoy these "Memoirs"*
*And Keep Them Close to Your Heart - Inside!*

*Lovingly!*

*aDc*
*04/03/92*

# No Pigs

I have no pigs to take to the auction
All I have are two silly dachshunds.
One is Sparky, the other is Precious
Both of them are definitely mischievous!

They delight me on a somber day
As they intrigue me in their own special way.
They sleep, they bark, they say, "I Love You"
Yes, they convey their thoughts, that true!

With both in my lap on a stormy day,
We chase the rumbling clouds away.
They're real and alive, no not a toy
They're my two dachshunds, my pride and joy.

aDc
04/18/2019

# My Son

On July 7, 1979, you came into my life
A precious little baby boy sent from God above
With eyes so big and bright
And a tiny heart so full of love.

You're growing so fast, I can't believe
The time will come and you'll be gone.
And next a young man with much to see
Adventures you seek on your own.

Now an adult with much to learn
With troubles and trials and snares
But do not fret nor be concerned
'Cause God is with you and He cares.

Just follow your heart, you'll be alright
Dreams do come true you'll see
Though the road get tough, no end in sight
Look next to you, that's where I'll be.

Don't ever get so far away
That you feel abandoned by the One above
He's the One who will have the final say
Yes, He's the One with eternal love.

aDc
04/18/2019

# My Melody

You're the song in my head, the breeze in my hair
I turn around so quickly so I can see you there.
But much to my surprise, you're already gone
And once again I missed you and seem to be alone.

I lost you once my baby girl, I can't do that again
I know you're watching from sites not yet known to man.
I hear the rustle of angel wings and a touch upon my face
So sweet it would be to feel your warm embrace.

Remember mama loves you and knows that you're alright
So, lay upon my shoulder before you take your flight.
Come back my angel and stay a little while
Let me gaze into your eyes and see your beautiful smile.

I miss you oh so much, it hurts down deep inside
The day you left so suddenly, a part of me just died.
I know you're free from all the ugly hurt and pain
But some day I know within my heart, we'll be together again!

I LOVE YOU MELODY

aDc
04/18/2019

# The Wedding Dress

Once worn on a special day
It was her dream come true, she'd say
Dressed as a princess with an enchanting smile
Ready to be escorted down the aisle.

It was special with the satin and lace
With glistening veil to hide her face.
Embroidered flowers on the bodice lay
Pearls and sequins that twinkled away.

Just a dress to some they say
But, oh, it's worn on this certain day.
Just some glitter and lace it seems
Yet it fulfills someone's treasured dream.

It now is carefully stored away
Seems it's turned a shade of grey.
Never to be worn again you see
Time to close this memory.

aDc 04/20/2019

# You're Just Away

Hi mom and dad! Just want to say hello
We miss you so much and want you to know
We send our love, our thoughts and prayers
One day we'll meet you up there.

The days go by and time passes on,
But the memories of you are forever strong.
Your faces are clear - your wonderful smiles
Those eyes so tender, the hearts of a child.

Your outreached hands in times of need,
Always offering to do a good deed.
The goodness we shared, our ups and our downs
It's not the same without you around.

And many hard times you did share
It's true you both made quite a pair.
All these thoughts will forever stay
As we remind ourselves...
You're no gone, You're just away.

aDc
04/19/2019

# The Medal

I'm sitting my classroom on a sunny day
And the teacher approaches in a quiet way.
She informs us of a new contest,
I was eager to join, I must confess.

So off to the drawing board I did go
My work, I was eager to show.
It happened to be "Fire Safety Week"
I drew some safety measures for all to seek.

Then a little poem and dropped the poster off.
The teacher read my entry, she didn't even scoff.
It was entered in the contest, I was nervous as could be
I thought no way would they choose me.

But much to my surprise, the choice had been settled
I won the price – a little golden medal!
So off to home with my prize of "gold"
In my hand, I would tightly hold.

aDc
04/18/2019

# The Arrival of Spring

As I venture outside to gaze at the dawn of a new day
My eyes catch the squirrels and red robins busily at play.
They hide away in the limbs of an old willow tree
Where they can nap under the sky of crisp clouds so free.

And the wildflowers in the meadow are damped with dew
Among the green grass that grows so strong and new.
Yet, I can breathe the fragrance of a bouquet of sweet, perfumed petals
As the pollen of spring finally begins to settle.

aDc<br>04/21/2019

# Faded Memories

Today the sunshine rests upon my face
And the good Lord above shows me His grace.
I'm still the same as sure as I can be
But something is different I cannot see.

My family is with me, I know them not
Oh my, it seems that I forgot.
Their names are on the tip of my tongue
But my days go back to when they were young.

The memories are fading though they seem
To be captured in a distant dream.
My constant thoughts seem engraved in stone
Makes me wonder what's going on.

I think I'm losing my mind no doubt
I don't understand what it is all about.
Just forgetfulness from growing old???
No, it's more than that, I'm told.

These memories get worse has the days go by
Somedays I feel alone, but don't know why.
These feelings leave me frightened you see
As my mind can't remember this person inside of me.

*Tribute to my mom who passed away with Alzheimer's. God bless all those who have connections to anyone with this disease. Just be patient and understand their present situation and love them as a little child.*

aDc 04/22/2019

# Tiny Little Footprints

Tiny little footprints, walking in the sand
Walking right beside him, holding mama's hand.
Such a pleasant sight for eyes to see
Walking so playfully - carelessly and free.

Then a swarm of waves quickly rush in
Retaining the level of sand again.
Washing away his presence there
Of tiny feet so fragile and bare.

All along the sandy beach the prints do go
And once again they will show.
When tides go out, they're gone away
But anxiously awaiting another day.

So off again to walk in the sand
And grasp a hold of mama's hand.
Maybe the waves will be good this time
And leave these tiny footprints of mine!

aDc
04/25/2019

# The Shadowbox

I learned a long, long time ago
That memories really needed to show.
So, the making of a shadowbox to view
Was made with something old, something new.

A lock of hair I placed within,
A favorite locket and a pin.
A little embroidery of the character – Eeyore
A lacy pillow from an event before.

All placed within the box to see
Resting in my cabinet bought for me.
With a loving heart, I bid you adieu
These precious memories are just a few.

To share these with those who seek
To view upon it and take a peek.
Enjoy the treasures within this box
It's one of a kind, it's out of stock.

aDc
04/25/2019

# The Birds and Bees

Let me tell you a story
That was oh so new to me.
A story that will blow your mind
And maybe some secrets you will find.

My little girl was ready to show me what she knew
Exactly what she had in mind, I didn't have a clue.
It seems they studied in daycare that day
The story of nature – didn't know what she would say!

"Mama, do you know the story of birds and bees?" she asked
I thought of my inevitable task.
I told her yes, my dear?
But you can explain it in your way that's clear.

Well she continued to explain to me about the birds and the bees
"You see, mama, the birds go tweet, tweet and the bees go bzzzzzzz."
This innocent explanation had surely made my day
She had the perfect ending in a perfect way!

aDc
04/25/2019

# Childhood Games

It's not unusual to see today's child at play
Sitting in front of a video game all day.
They know not the thrills of Hide 'N Seek
And closing your eyes, don't you dare to peek.

Or playing cowboys and Indians around the big tree
Where you were the cowboy and the Indian was me.
Me with my arrows and you with your guns
We would try to catch each other but, oh, how we run.

With a broom stick for our horse
We'd gallop with all our force.
After chasing each other for what seemed like a mile
We would claim a truce and just rest a while.

Then on to bigger and better things
Like an old tire made into a swing.
Or hop scotch with nine squares to jump
Or, maybe a tea party given at lunch.

Yes, it's true the times have changed
No one plays my childhood games.

aDC
04/26/2019

# Abigail

While walking in the hall of work one day
I noticed a tractor with a web out a window bay
The author was working in the morning dew
As she wove the web so beautiful and new.

So, I took a picture of the web and the tractor
As pretty as it was, that wasn't the main factor.
You see, I had caught a glimpse of something so bright
That left an outline of heavenly light.

I thought when I saw it, it was an odd sight
But I had captured my angel taking flight.
Nothing around to make that reflection
No overcast of clouds to my recollection.

Her graceful wings spread out to show
Her flight from here she must go.
A stream of light pushing her up and away
I had met my guardian angel, Abigail, that day.

aDc
04/26/2019

# A House...A Home

You can build yourself a big, fancy house
Filled with nails and two by fours.
A roof to keep the rains out
And beautiful wooden floors.

You can add a sofa and a chair
And a kitchen to keep the family fed.
Then some pictures covering up the walls so bare
Now a big, oak bed to rest your weary head.

You can add a family – a mom and a dad
And children to fill each room.
But without the love, it would be so sad
This house would surely end in doom.

So, fill your house with lots of love
And see what it becomes
Count your blessings from above
You'll see your house becomes your Home.

aDc
04/26/2019

# The Quilt

There lays a covering on my grandma's bed
With a history behind it . . . it is said.
The young ladies use to gather and sew
And learn the gossip they didn't know.

Yes, it's true they'd have a quilting party
And their efforts were always quite hearty.
The patchwork squares were sewn that day
With cotton thread that would not fray.

A time of laughter to cry and to sing
Around the table, the quilt would bring.
A joyful peace for all who would gather
To remain as friends for ever and ever.

It seems the quilt was finished on time
To be a gift for someone so fine.
Tradition has it – a quilting party is said
To make a covering for a new bride's bed.

aDc
04/26/2019

# God's Messengers

Tiny Lil Angel sent with blessings from above,
To bring someone joy and fill their heart with love.
Bringing peace and tranquility to a troubled one,
Knowing not your mission until the job is done.

Tiny Lil Angel, you've come a long way
To help the weary through another long day.
You lift someone from a heavy load
You bring joy to someone sad it is told.

Tiny Lil Angel, you're such a pleasant sight to see
Your entertaining, joyful smile brings contentment to me.
I'm so glad you were sent to cheer me on
Otherwise, my days would be awfully long.

Tiny Lil Angel, you work with all your strife
You've brought a fulfillment to my life.
Thanks for the visit you made to me
I'll guard you gently, as gently as I can be.

aDc
04/27/2019

# Mockingbird Hollow

'Tis a beautiful morning in the country to see
The green, moist meadow is calling to me.
I can feel the glowing sun stroked across my face
And out of the corners of my eyes I see the rabbits and squirrels running
a race.

I noticed a sunlit river where children play
And a fisherman is steering a trout his way.
Yes, the buttercups and daisies are shadowed from the coral sun,
But the bees and butterflies are having their fun.

Two mothers smile while singing a song so sweet
As an eagle takes flight to find something to eat.
It's a paintbrush picture just waiting to paint
With treasured family and children so quaint.

Tis the end of the story of Mockingbird Hollow
The story has been written, just waiting for the picture to follow.

aDc
04/29/2019

# If I Was a Hummingbird

IF I was a hummingbird so happy and free
I'd buzz around anything red being drawn to me.
I'd be a loner so I could get more nectar
But if another comes around, I won't neglect her.

I would come when the weather is right
Sometimes I even fly in the rain and fly at night.
I'm fast like lightning so you have be quick to see
Don't try to catch me, don't think that will be.

You'll know when I'm around 'cause my wings just flutter
So don't be afraid and please don't shutter.
I'm a peaceful little bird, don't want no trouble
Just don't mess with my nectar in my bubble.

aDc
04/29/2019

# Love Is Blind

Love is blind some people will say
Guess it's too late, gave my heart away.
To someone so sweet, so gentle I thought
Too late, my love has already been sought.

A love so fragile lasted only a few years
Then the breakup, heartache and tears.
For the love I had found, found someone new
Leaving me alone, heart-broken and blue.

But as fate would have it, someone new came along
A God send from Heaven so gentle and strong.
"Love is blind," so some people did say
But it was too late, gave my heart away.

With many years of sweet married bliss
Now you're gone and, oh, I do miss.
The good times, your laughter, and your smile
You kept me happy for a long, long while.

You're entertaining the angels above
With your heart so big and full of love.
You see, Love is blind but it's just what you make
Give your heart away, it's a chance you take!

aDc
04/28/2019

# Patience

One day while working at my desk on matters from the heart
I got a call from someone who wanted to be a part.
We talked a long, long time, the offer sound so good
Took a blind leap of faith, didn't know where I stood.

Well, calls kept coming and conversations were long
The callers were persistant and the speeches were strong.
I kept on listening and saying "I don't know
The price is too steep for me to go."

The voices were so encouraging and truthful, you see
I'll help you, just trust me, so, let's let this be.
I finally said yes to the offer made
But now I'm feeling overwhelmed and afraid!

What if the items sells or maybe they won't
I'll be in a world of hurt and that I don't want.
Let's just take it slow with the process
Then let's see if the project is a success!

Then maybe on to bigger and better things
Maybe on to fulfilling my dream
Just give me some time, be patient with me
The future is out there, you will see!

aDc
05/02/2019

# The Heart Is In The Home

A home is where you lay your head
When you go to sleep at night.
You feel safe and warm within your bed
Away from fear and fright.

But in this universe so big and wide
Where ever you may roam
You can venture far and wide
But always look forward to coming home.

Whenever you're away and with a new home you are faced
Everything is as you need, everything in place.
But special memories just aren't there,
Like the sweet smell of roses that fill the room with grace.

So, no matter where you're apt to roam
There's really no place like home.
Be grateful to have a home so bliss
And remember, the heart is in the home.

aDc
05/08/2019

# Angel On The Highway

It had been an extremely odd day
On which I had met with Dr J.
You see I was having trouble with trust
And he told me it was really a must.
Easier said than done, I did say.

So on to home after work I decided to go
When around me a little, white car did blow.
With speed so fast, it seemed like a trick
But noticed a tag that read PROV 356.
Knew it was scripture, but what would it show?

I hurried home to read God's Word
To my eyes, it read "Trust in the Lord..."
Such an answer to my problem, I did see
I knew right then He was talking to me
An angel on the highway, I grew to adore.

Well after the 2nd visit with Dr. J
I had to build my trust was what he did say.
Told him I would if I saw another sign
And to miss it, I would have had to be blind,
There it was on the second weekly day.

Next come the 3rd visit with you know who
Again he stressed what I had to do.
And at a church sign it, too, did say
"Trust in the Lord... in all thy ways..."
This was not just some saying, it was true.

The words were clear and I could see
"All things aren't bad so you must believe,
Put your faith in God and learn to trust
You see, I had turned that reality from a must.
On the 4th visit it happen to me, a feeling of being free!

aDc
05/07/2019

# Camila

I have a friend in whom I can confide
My deepest secrets hidden inside.
She listens quite well and doesn't speak
The coversations she forever keeps.

She's tall and slender, a southern girl
With big brown eyes and a head full of curls.
Her lips are small, her skin so smooth
Her loyalty is most greatly approved.

She's dressed in linen and beautiful lace
And always fits in this time and place.
She'll never look old and never will evolve
She's Camila - my friend, my porcelain doll.

aDc
05/07/2019

# The Carousel

We met inside the entrance gate
Beside the concession stand.
The theme of the carnival was so exciting
And the crowds were engaged in tent games.
As we walked, my ear caught a catchy tune
Coming from the center attraction.
There it was - a beautiful carousel
With many colorful animals on poles.
But no one was on board to enjoy it.
So, we stepped upon the wooded floor
And gazed upon the animals there.
I mounted a white horse - he mounted grey
They started dancing up and down.
And for a while I was dreaming of a time
When life was fun, and calm with no worries.
Being a child again was delightfully fresh
Suddenly I was awakened by a stop so soon.
Back to reality, time to exit my place
And face the world once again!

aDc
05/07/2019

# The 4th of July

It's the 4th of July and a carnival's in town
With lots of games and a merry-go-round.
It's tune is very mellow and sweet
But every now and then, there's an awful squeak.

Next is a big tent filled with animals galore
With elephants and monkeys and lions that roar.
Also, a clown with huge, big toes
And a horn that honks when he touches his nose.

There comes a marching band through the crowd here
And all the bystanders let out a cheer!
The trumpets sound off so very loudly
Then the rest of the band join in so proudly.

All of a sudden five jets soar over the crowd
Leaving trails of smoke out of engines so loud.
That's right – it's the 4th of July at Disney's Revue
Making it special for little ones like you.

aDc
05/09/2019

# Index